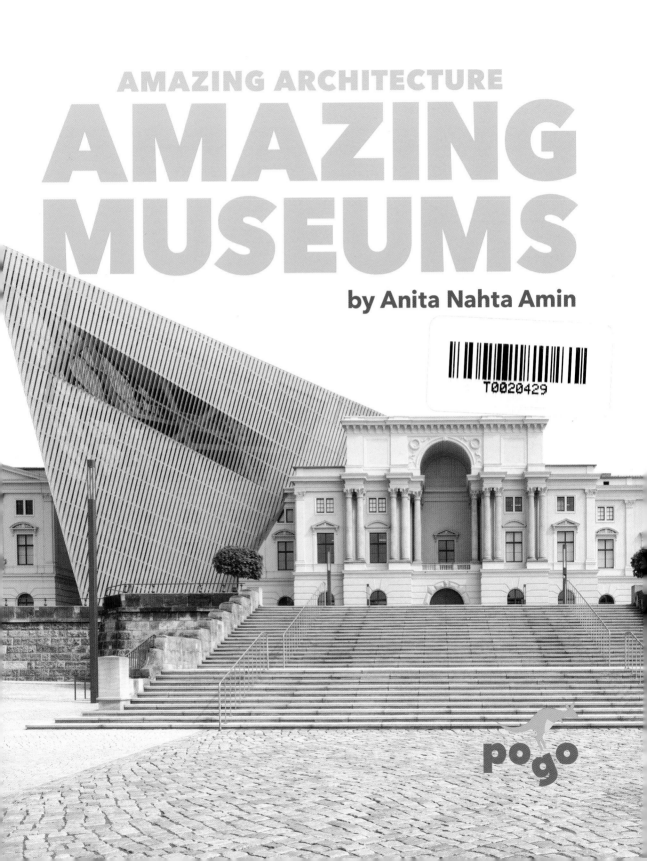

AMAZING ARCHITECTURE
AMAZING MUSEUMS

by Anita Nahta Amin

pogo

Ideas for Parents and Teachers

Pogo Books let children practice reading informational text while introducing them to nonfiction features such as headings, labels, sidebars, maps, and diagrams, as well as a table of contents, glossary, and index.

Carefully leveled text with a strong photo match offers early fluent readers the support they need to succeed.

Before Reading

- "Walk" through the book and point out the various nonfiction features. Ask the student what purpose each feature serves.
- Look at the glossary together. Read and discuss the words.

Read the Book

- Have the child read the book independently.
- Invite him or her to list questions that arise from reading.

After Reading

- Discuss the child's questions. Talk about how he or she might find answers to those questions.
- Prompt the child to think more. Ask: What kinds of museums have you been to? What types of architecture did they have?

Pogo Books are published by Jump!
5357 Penn Avenue South
Minneapolis, MN 55419
www.jumplibrary.com

Library of Congress Cataloging-in-Publication Data

Names: Amin, Anita Nahta, author.
Title: Amazing museums / by Anita Nahta Amin.
Description: Minneapolis, MN: Jump!, Inc., [2023]
Series: Amazing architecture
Includes index. | Audience: Ages 7-10
Identifiers: LCCN 2021062969 (print)
LCCN 2021062970 (ebook)
ISBN 9781636907383 (hardcover)
ISBN 9781636907390 (paperback)
ISBN 9781636907406 (ebook)
Subjects: LCSH: Museum architecture–Juvenile literature. Museum buildings–Juvenile literature.
Classification: LCC NA6690 .A48 2023 (print)
LCC NA6690 (ebook) | DDC 727/.6–dc23/eng/20220222
LC record available at https://lccn.loc.gov/2021062969
LC ebook record available at https://lccn.loc.gov/2021062970

Editor: Eliza Leahy
Designer: Molly Ballanger

Photo Credits: Ken Wolter/Shutterstock, cover; Nessa Gnatoush/Shutterstock, 1; HasanZaidi/Shutterstock, 3; Gala Images/age fotostock/SuperStock, 4; ABCDstock/Shutterstock, 5; Robert Landau/Alamy, 6-7; naskami/Shutterstock, 8; Christopher Sharpe/Shutterstock, 9; Alex Segre/Shutterstock, 10-11; Renato Meireles/Dreamstime, 12; Luciano Lozano Raya/Getty, 13; Annimei/iStock, 14-15; Michael Mulkens/Shutterstock, 16-17; Elenaphotos/Dreamstime, 18-19; Roy Harris/Shutterstock, 19; Rob Crandall/Shutterstock, 20-21; Firebird007/Shutterstock, 23.

Printed in the United States of America at Corporate Graphics in North Mankato, Minnesota.

Title Page Image: Bundeswehr Military History Museum, Germany

TABLE OF CONTENTS

National Museum
of Qatar

CHAPTER 1

WHAT YOU SEE IS WHAT YOU GET

The Weisman Art Museum in Minneapolis, Minnesota, looks like a **sculpture**. Cubes, cones, and **cylinders** pop out from its walls.

Weisman Art Museum

Museums often look like what they feature on the inside. The Shanghai Astronomy Museum in China is all about outer space. So the museum was built to look like it!

model

Architects design museums. They start with **blueprints**. They build **models**. Then, **engineers** and construction workers build the museums.

DID YOU KNOW?

Some museums have **themes**, such as art or nature. Some are for certain kinds of people. Children's museums help children learn.

CHAPTER 2

AIR, LIGHT, AND LOAD

Museums need to be strong. Their floors must hold the **load** of everything on them. Walls, **columns**, and arches support each floor.

arch

column

glass case

Museums hold special items. They help **preserve** them. Glass cases keep air out. Why? Objects can melt or crack if they get too hot. Damp air can also damage items. Dirty air can turn them yellow.

Sunlight fades colors. Camera lights and light bulbs do, too. Special **filters** are on museum windows and overhead lights. Window shades block sunlight.

NO FLASH PHOTOGRAPHY!

Thank you.

TAKE A LOOK!

How do shades, filters, and glass cases protect special items? Take a look!

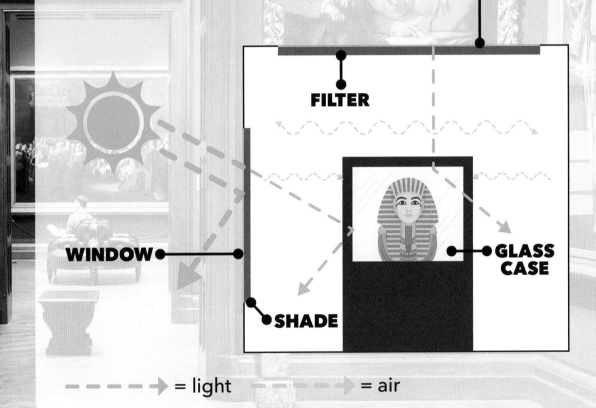

LIGHT BULB

FILTER

WINDOW

GLASS CASE

SHADE

- - - → = light   - - - → = air

CHAPTER 3

FAMOUS MUSEUMS

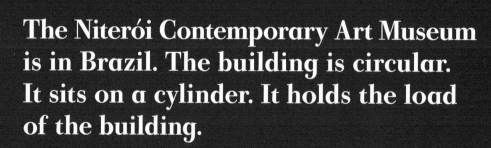

cylinder

The Niterói Contemporary Art Museum is in Brazil. The building is circular. It sits on a cylinder. It holds the load of the building.

Windows on the upper levels look out to the ocean.

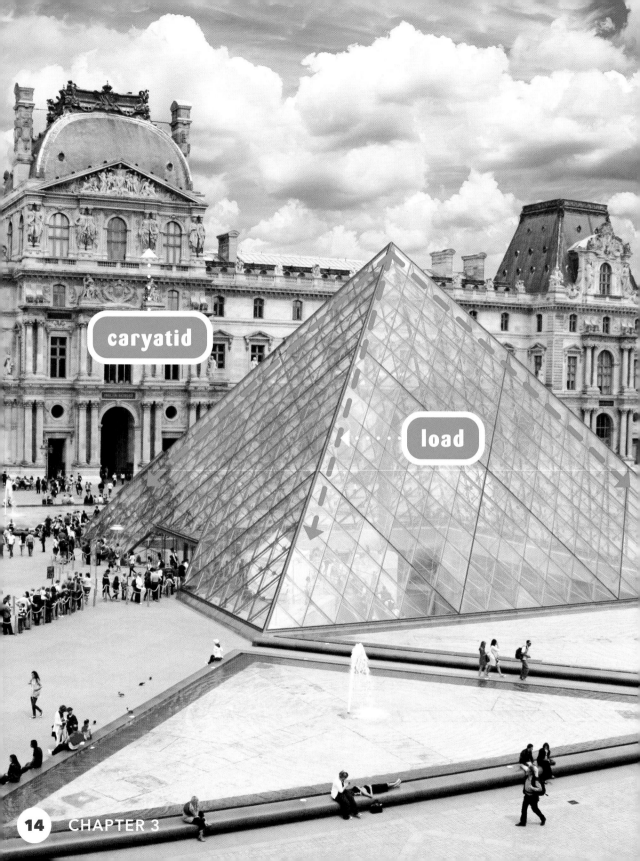

caryatid

load

The Louvre Museum is in Paris, France. It is the largest art museum in the world. Arches and columns support it.

Glass **pyramids** let light in. The largest one makes up the main entrance. It is 71 feet (22 meters) tall. The load pushes down the sides.

DID YOU KNOW?

Some of the Louvre's columns are caryatids. These are statues of women. They help support the building.

Centre Pompidou in Paris is inside out. How? Its pipes are on the outside. Escalators and elevators are, too. So is the steel grid that supports the building. This leaves more space on the inside. There, you can find a museum, a library, and more!

steel grid

web wall ·····▶

skylight

The Guggenheim is in New York City. Its Frank Lloyd Wright building has a spiral ramp. Its **dome** skylight is 58 feet (18 m) across. It is made up of 12 parts. Each part sits on a web wall. These hold the building up.

Guggenheim

Part of the Smithsonian's National Museum of African American History and Culture is underground. The upper levels are shaped like **trapezoids**.

Take a look at your local museum. What parts do you see?

trapezoid

ACTIVITIES & TOOLS

COLOR FADE

Museums control light to protect important items. See how sunlight fades color in this fun activity!

What You Need:
- a piece of black or dark-colored paper
- an opaque object, such as a coaster or lid, that does not let light through
- a pencil

1. Put the piece of paper in a bright, sunny spot.

2. Place the object in the middle of the paper. It should not cover the whole paper. If it does, choose a smaller object.

3. Use the pencil to trace the object.

4. Leave the object on the paper and in the sun for one hour.

5. After an hour, remove the object from the piece of paper. Is the spot that was under the object darker or the same color as the rest of the paper?

6. Put the object back in its spot on the paper. Repeat Steps 4 and 5 every hour for a few hours. What do you notice about the color of the paper each time?

architects: People who design the look of structures.

blueprints: Models or detailed sketches of how structures will look.

columns: Pillars that help support structures.

complex: A group of buildings that are near each other and are used for similar purposes.

cylinders: Shapes with flat, circular ends and sides shaped like the outside of a tube.

dome: A roof shaped like half of a sphere.

engineers: People who are specially trained to design and build machines or large structures.

filters: Devices that absorb light.

load: The amount carried at one time.

models: Things architects or engineers build or design as examples of larger structures.

preserve: To protect something so that it stays in its original or current state.

pyramids: Solid shapes with square bases and triangular sides that meet at the tops.

sculpture: Something carved or shaped out of stone, wood, marble, or clay or cast in bronze or another metal.

themes: Main subjects or topics of art, writing, speeches, or exhibitions.

trapezoids: Shapes that have four sides of which only two are parallel.

Messner Mountain Museum, Italy

INDEX

TO LEARN MORE

Finding more information is as easy as 1, 2, 3.

1. **Go to www.factsurfer.com**

2. **Enter "amazingmuseums" into the search box.**

3. **Choose your book to see a list of websites.**

FACT SURFER